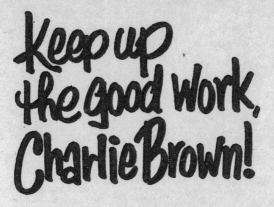

Keep up the good work, Charlie Brown!

by CHARLES M. SCHULZ

Selected Cartoons from
SPEAK SOFTLY, AND CARRY A BEAGLE, Vol. III

FAWCETT CREST • NEW YORK

A Fawcett Crest Book
Published by Ballantine Books

Contents of Book: PEANUTS® comic strips by Charles M.
Schulz
Copyright © 1975 by United Feature Syndi-
cate, Inc.

ISBN 0-449-20405-7

This book comprises a portion of SPEAK SOFTLY, AND
CARRY & BEAGLE, and is reprinted by arrangement with
Holt, Rinehart and Winston.

Printed in Canada

First Fawcett Crest Edition: November 1978
First Ballantine Books Edition: April 1983

Keep up the good work, Charlie Brown!

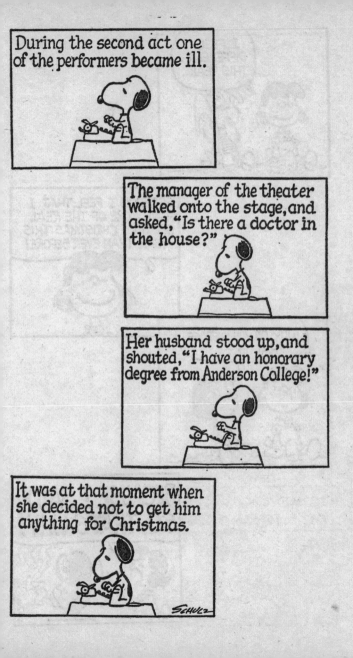

HERE COMES WOODSTOCK ON HIS NEW BICYCLE...
I HATE IT WHEN HE SAYS, "LOOK, NO WINGS!"
SCHULZ

Gentlemen,
I ordered a toy bicycle for my sister's doll set.
It was supposed to be here by Christmas. Perhaps it was delivered to the wrong address.
Would you look into the matter, please? Thank you.
I REFUSE TO BE THE ONE WHO TELLS HIM!
SCHULZ

THE SNOW GODS
HATE ME!

SCHULZ

SNOOPY! WHY DON'T YOU COME INTO THE HOUSE, AND I'LL FEED YOU HERE? IT'S A LOT WARMER!
HOW NICE... AN INVITATION TO DINNER..
TAP
TAP
TAP
WHY DOES HE HAVE TO MAKE A BIG DEAL OUT OF EVERYTHING?
SCHULZ

IT'S NEVER TOO EARLY TO CHECK YOUR MAILBOX FOR VALENTINES..
BUT FOR SAFETY'S SAKE, IT'S A GOOD IDEA TO STAND WAY BACK IN CASE A FLOOD OF VALENTINES COMES POURING OUT...
SIGH
SCHULZ